Sea and Motion Sickness

Description
Motion, Sea, Space, Car, Airplane
and Virtual Environment Sickness.
Causes, Treatment and Prevention.

By Anton Swanepoel

Copyright © 2014 Anton Swanepoel
All rights reserved. No part of this publication may be reproduced, distributed, or transmitted in any form or by any means, or stored in a database or retrieval system, without the prior written permission of the author.
Amazon Kindle ASIN: B006YLKKKY
Print ISBN- 10: 1467934534
Print ISBN- 13: 978-1467934534
Smashwords ISBN: 9781310871788
All rights reserved.

www.antonswanepoelbooks.com
http://www.facebook.com/AuthorAntonSwanepoel
https://twitter.com/Author_Anton

Introduction

With the earth being in constant motion, it is strange that humans suffer from motion sickness. Millions of people travel across the globe daily; by land, sea and air. Many of these travelers suffer from motion sickness, from mild and irritating, to extreme sickness and immobility.

In this book, we will look at what motion sickness is, space sickness, virtual environment sickness, and sea sickness, their causes and triggers, with advice for preventing and treating them.

Welcome to trouble free motion

Books by Anton

All books are available for sale on Author's website; in Mobi, Epub, PDF, and Print form.

Sign up and receive news on new releases and book promotions.

www.antonswanepoelbooks.com

Laura and The Jaguar Prophecy (Book 1)
Laura and The God Code (Book 2)
Laura and the Spear of Destiny (Book 3)

Machu Picchu Doing It Yourself
The Art of Travel
Taking on The Road, Two Wheels at a Time
Angkor Wat & Cambodia
Vietnam Caves
Kampot, Kep and Sihanoukville
Motorbiking Cambodia & Vietnam

Dive Computers
Gas Blender Program
Deep and Safety Stops, and Gradient Factors
Diving Below 130 Feet
The Art of Gas Blending

Writing and Publishing Your Own Book

Ear Pain
Sea and Motion Sickness

About the Author

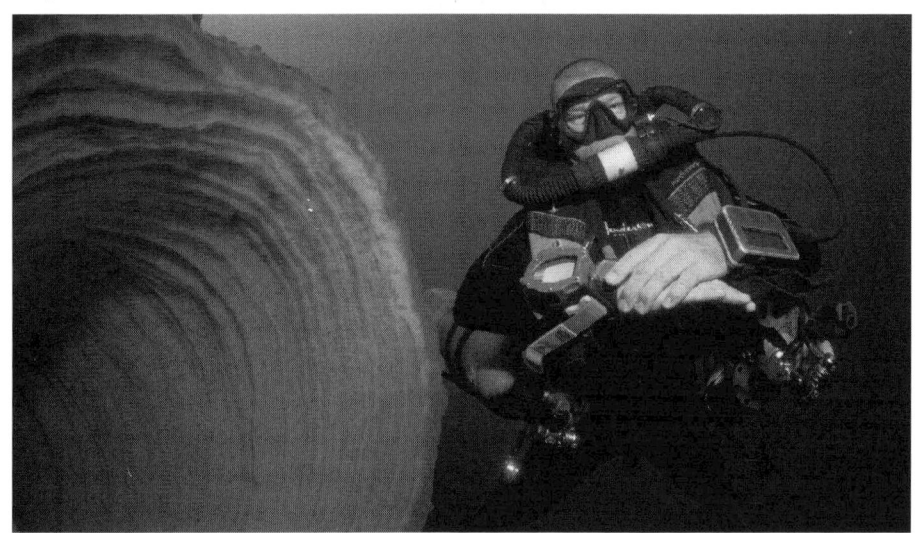

Author at 200ft. Cayman Islands, Grand Cayman.
Photo taken by Robert Hew

Anton Swanepoel is a diving instructor for IANTD, TDI, NAUI and PADI. He is an OC Tri-Mix instructor and a Tri-Mix gas blender instructor. He has a passion for wreck, cave and deep diving and has done OC dives to over 400 ft.

Anton loves to research topics of interest to him and write about it. As he himself suffers from motion sickness, and has seen many students and divers suffer from motion sickness, he decided to research deeper into the subject in order to find out more about the causes and possible cures.

What he found is that there is not that much known about the subject by the general public and that most information is contradicting or wrong. Sea and motion sickness seems to also be a bigger problem than just divers getting sick, as dogs and cats going for a ride suffer the same fate as humans. The result of his research is this book.

Disclaimer

Note that even though the advice in this book has been sourced from diving doctors, specialists, DAN (Divers Alert Network), medical facilities and medical websites, the author is not a medical professional and the information in this book is thus for information purposes only. Always consult with a medical specialist or your doctor before taking any medication or following any advice.

The author does not give out medical advice. The author accepts no responsibility for any advice given in this book. Readers are to use their own discretion in following any advice and accept all risk onto themselves for following any advice given in this book.

Do know that motion sickness is triggered differently in each person, as to the degree of emotion needed to trigger the onset of symptoms. There is no one solution for all, but a variety of different options, one can try to manage and reduce the symptoms and possibly increase the amount of motion needed before symptoms are realized. This book contains a number of options currently available, I hope one works for you as some did for me. However, you may need multiple solutions together if you get sick easily.

Table of Contents

Chapter 1: What is motion sickness? 11
What is motion sickness? 11
Who is affected by it? 11

Chapter 2: Motions sickness symptoms 13
Motions sickness symptoms 13

Chapter 3: Is motion sickness a serious condition? .. 14
Is motion sickness a serious condition? 14
When you should see a doctor 14

Chapter 4: How our sense of balance works 16
How our sense of balance works 16
The inner ears (also called the labyrinth) 17
The eyes 18
Skin pressure receptors 18
Muscle and joint sensory receptors 18
The central nervous system (CNS) 18

Chapter 5: Causes of motion sickness 19
Causes of motion sickness 19
Sensory conflict 19
Two different types of Neural Mismatch 20
Visual–vestibular conflict 20
Type 1 subdivision 20
Type 2 subdivision 21
Intra vestibular (Canal–otolith) conflict 21
Type 1 subdivision 21
Type 2 A subdivision 22
Positional alcohol vertigo (PAV) 23
Benign paroxysmal vertigo (BPV) 23
Type 2 B subdivision 23
Poison response 24

Simulator Sickness *24*
Virtual reality systems *25*
Space motion sickness *26*
Trains and motion sickness *27*
Motion sickness vs sea sickness *28*
Putting it all together *29*
Additional theories *30*
Conclusion *30*

Chapter 6: Preventing and treating motion sickness *31*

Preventing and treating motion sickness *31*
Natural build up *32*
Acupressure and acustimulation *33*
Behavior modification techniques (biofeedback) *34*
Exercises for motion sickness *35*
Ginger *35*
Against Ginger *36*
For Ginger *38*
Why ginger is thought to work *39*
Conclusion on ginger *39*
Side effects of ginger *40*
Drugs *40*
Promethazine (Phenergan®), (Pentazine) *41*
Scopolamine-dextroamphetamine *41*
Scopolamine patch (Trans-Derm SCOP®) *42*
Metoclopramide (Metozolv ODT, Reglan) *43*
Ondansetron (Zofran) *43*
Dilantin® *43*
Dimenhydrinate (Dramamine®), Driminate *44*
Meclizine (Bonine®), (Antivert®), D-Vert, Dramamine II *44*
Cyclizine (Marezine®) *45*
Diphenhydramine *45*
Haldol, Thorazine and Diazepam (valium) *45*
Diazepam (valium), Lorazepam and Klonazepam *45*
Alprazolam (Niravam, Xanax, Xanax XR) *46*
Prochlorperazine (Compazine) *46*
Note on drugs for motion sickness *46*

Other medication *47*
Verapamil *47*
Phenytoin and Carbamazepine *47*
Buspirone (Buspar) *47*
Herbal treatments *48*
DizzyStop's® *48*
CanTravel™ *48*
Trip ease *48*
MotionEaze *49*
Hyland's Motion Sickness *50*
On The Move *50*
Small snacks *50*
Fluids *51*
Find a calm spot *51*
Get fresh air *52*
Cephalic vagal reflex *52*
Electronic wrist band *53*
Pressure point wristband (Seaband) *55*
Peppermint *55*
Ice water *56*
Coca-Cola and Pepsi *56*
Hypnosis and self-hypnosis *56*
Subliminal messages *57*
Changing your handwriting *57*

Chapter 7: Tips for preventing motion sickness *59*
Tips for preventing motion sickness *59*

Chapter 8: Vomit in your regulator or not? *64*
Vomit in your regulator or not? *64*
If you have to *64*
Taking the regulator out *65*
Keep the regulator in *65*
Swap regulators *65*

Chapter 9: Motion sickness and animals *67*
  Motion sickness and animals *67*

Chapter 10: Tips for scuba divers *69*
  Tips for scuba divers *69*

End Note *73*

Resources *74*

Other Books by this Author *75*

Chapter 1

What is motion sickness?

The term 'motion sickness' (also known as Kinetosis) refers to a collection of symptoms that can occur in both humans and animals after exposure to a real or illusory motion, often equated with nausea and vomiting.

Note that motion sickness is not actually a sickness, just a normal response from the body to unfamiliar motion. Motion sickness has been recorded in ancient Greek times, and interestingly the English word "nausea" comes from the Greek word for ship (naus), also the origin of the word "nautical".

Even though motion sickness has been studied for years by many agencies such as NASA, USAF and a number of universities, the causes and remedies are still not completely understood. This is mostly due to conflicting results from studies done in preventing motion sickness. However, tests reveal that repetitive motion (such as boat, air and car travel) causes the hypothalamus, pons and the medulla Oblongata to produce excess levels of histamines that is associated with motion sickness symptoms. The medulla is thought to be the brain's vomiting center.

Who is affected by it?

Any persons with normal vestibular function can get sick with the right conditions, however susceptibility to motion sickness differs from person to person and even from day to day. When talking about motion sickness, many people think only of humans being affected, however animals suffer from motion sickness as well. Dogs and cats suffer the same fate as humans when it comes to traveling. Not even astronauts are safe, approximately 70% of all crew members experience motion sickness to a degree during the first 72 hours of an orbital flight on a space shuttle.

People who have lost total vestibular function (balance control in the ear) are normally immune to motion sickness, and people who suffered partial vestibular function loss are less susceptible. From large studies done, all people in a life raft in heavy seas will succumb to motion sickness to some degree.

Women are reported to be more susceptible to motion sickness, and a study done by Ramsay in 1994 and later by Grunfeld and Gresty in 1999 found that women at 9-15 days of the menstrual cycle appear to have a higher incidence of nausea, although some tests done by others did not have the same findings.

From tests done, it is shown that susceptibility to motion sickness increases with age until about 12 years of age, although infants and babies up to the age of two years old rarely suffer from motion sickness. Between the ages of four years and 12 years old, susceptibility to motion sickness increases to where it reaches a peak. After reaching its peak, susceptibility gradually starts to decline as tolerance to motion sickness slowly increases, thus with increasing age, sensitivity to motion sickness declines.

However, it should be noted that the decline is based on your own susceptibility to motion sickness, even though you may be less susceptible the older you get, if you were highly susceptible as a child, you will still be greatly affected by motion compared to other people that were less susceptible as children. Thus elderly people are not immune to motion sickness, just less susceptible compared to when they were younger.

Chapter 2

Motions sickness symptoms

The first symptoms of motion sickness are normally "head signs" such as headaches (migraines included), light-headedness, a general feeling of discomfort (malaise), drowsiness, yawning, strange taste in the mouth (can be metal taste), dryness in the mouth or increased salivation, and visual symptoms. The sufferer may feel hot and in need of cooling off, while others experience skin flushing (Vasodilation) or cold sweating. Sopite syndrome (sleepiness caused by motion, rocking the baby to sleep) is also a common symptom.

More severe symptoms are normally "gut signs", such as a general feeling of unwell, nausea and vomiting, depression, anxiety, confusion, sweating and dismay. Symptoms may only be mild and unpleasant; however for some people it can totally incapacitate them where they are unable to perform any functions at all.

Most people feel better after vomiting, however symptoms may return if exposure to motion that induced motion sickness is continued. Symptoms can last for days, such as when caught in rough weather or in space flight, however most people start to build up some tolerance after two to three days of continued exposure to such conditions.

In some people (normally those being afraid of the environment they are in) hyperventilation may be seen which can lead to panic.

Chapter 3

Is motion sickness a serious condition?

Motion sickness in itself is not normally a problem; however the symptoms can cause problems for an individual depending on the environment they are in. For example, if you are diving and become sick underwater, it is more dangerous than if you are on the boat, as breathing and vomiting does not go so well together when you are underwater.

In addition, if you are in control of a vehicle or airplane, then it can have serious consequences if you become incapacitated from motion sickness. The symptoms (such as nausea and vomiting) normally resolve in a few hours after exposure to motion sickness conditions are ended, however some people have reported some symptoms for up to a week. Lingering symptoms are normally called disembarkment or arrival sickness.

Note that continued vomiting can lead to dehydration and electrolyte abnormalities.

When you should see a doctor

Although motion sickness is normally self-treatable using either natural products such as ginger and peppermint, or commercial products such as wristbands or over the counter drugs, there are cases where these options do not work.

If the normal option does not work for you, or if the symptoms continue or become progressively worse, then it is time to see a doctor. This would also include cases where motion sickness symptoms such as dizziness and nausea are present without any apparent reason, such as experiencing it on dry land (playing video games excluded).

Note that prolonged vomiting can lead to dehydration, metabolic alkalosis (a metabolic condition where the pH of tissue elevates beyond the normal range), and hypokalaemia (a lower than normal amount of potassium in the blood that can be life threatening).

For people with severe symptoms and vomiting, normal oral medication is normally ineffective as the absorption dosage is impaired by the gastrointestinal tract due to gastric stasis and emesis. For these individuals intramuscular injections of promethazine or scopolamine (25–30 mg) is normally the preferred treatment.

Another method is rectal suppositories of promethazine and cyclizine.

Chapter 4

How our sense of balance works

Due to the balance and equilibrium system being largely involved in motion sickness, it helps to know a little about how we stay in balance.

The balance system is often called sense spatial orientation due to it informing the brain of where the body is in a 3D environment, "space". The information relayed to the brain includes many signals, such as the direction we are facing, the direction the body is in motion to, the tilt of the head, the position of each limb, and if we are upside down or upright. All this information helps the body to adjust to our changing environment to keep us in balance.

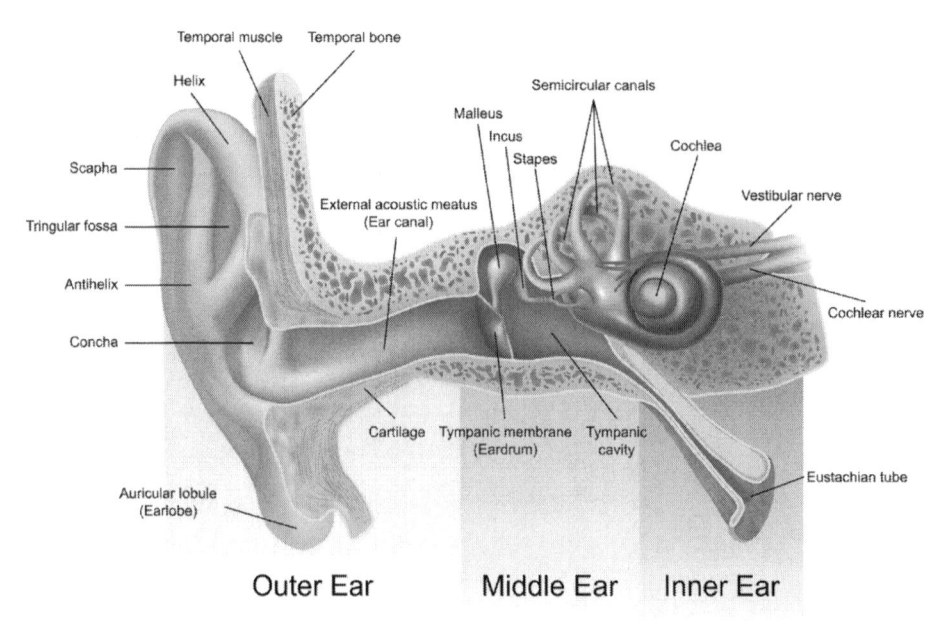

Structure of the ear

Some of the parts of the nervous system that help in maintaining our balance and sending signals to the brain are:

1: The inner ears (also called the labyrinth).
The inner ear is responsible for sensing the direction of motion and the tilt of the head, including our position in space, such as if we are falling or not, if we are turning, going forward or backwards, and if we are going to one side or the other. Inside the ears are three semicircular canals that each contain a small calcium deposit called otoliths (ear stones). As you move, these little stones move, sending the corresponding signals to your brain. The inner ear also contains the vestibule, the central part of the osseous labyrinth, situated behind the cochlea and in front of the semicircular canals. Within the cochlea are three fluid-filled spaces; the scala tympani, the scala vestibuli and the scala media, they sense motion and send the signals to the brain.

The semicircular canals provides angular information, the otoliths (utricule and saccule) provide multi-directional linear information. The receptors in the ampulla of each semicircular duct are stimulated by angular accelerations while the receptors in the utricular and saccular maculae (otolith organs) are stimulated by linear accelerations.

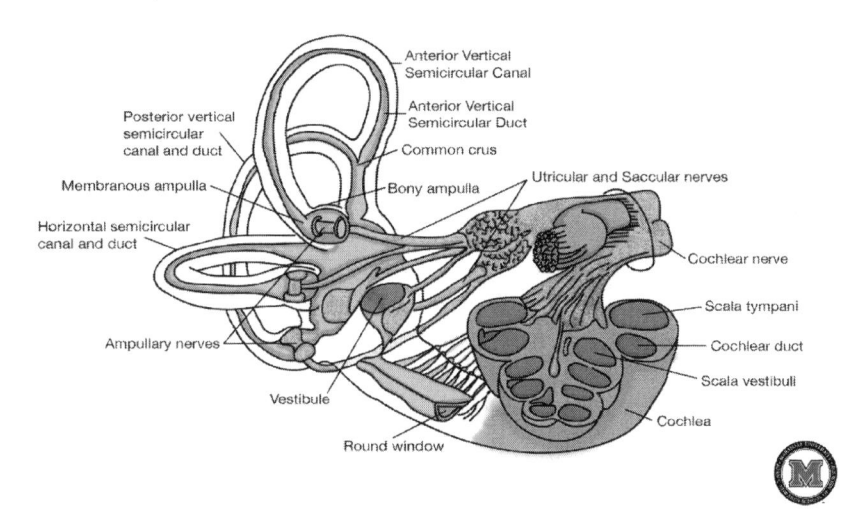

2: The eyes.
The eyes send visual cues to the brain to inform the brain of our changing environment and our placement in it, such as our movement in it, forward, backwards, upside-down and falling. This information should match what the inner ears are experiencing.

3: Skin pressure receptors.
There are numerous skin pressure receptors on the body such as on the soles of your feet and palms of your hands. The signals from them help to inform the brain on what part of the body is in contact with its environment.

4: Muscle and joint sensory receptors.
The muscle and joint sensory receptors send information to the brain on what parts of the body are moving, such as when walking, when a leg goes out forward, or if you are hanging from a bar doing acrobatics and swing to grab a different bar.

5: The central nervous system (CNS).
The CNS includes the brain and spinal cord and is the hub of all the processing of the different signals received from the four other systems. From here signals are then sent back to the body to coordinate movement to keep the body in balance.

Chapter 5

Causes of motion sickness

Currently, the exact cause of motion sickness is not fully understood. There are some theories, mostly based on observation and testing.

Sensory conflict

One theory is that motion sickness is the result of sensory conflict (originally proposed by Reason and Brand (1975)), such as between the vestibular system and vision system. Probst and Schmidt (1998) investigated two types of mismatch, namely vestibular-vestibular mismatch, and visual-vestibular mismatch. The brain senses motion through three different pathways of the nervous system, each sending signals as to its own experience of motion, these are the inner ear (sensing motion, acceleration, and gravity), the eyes (vision), and the deeper tissues of the body surface (proprioceptors). When these signals mismatch (called a neuron mismatch), the brain has difficulty in processing the information, causing motion sickness.

The neuron mismatch is thought to involve levels of the neurotransmitter histamine, acetylcholine, and norepinephrine, and as such many of the anti-motion sickness drugs used today work by influencing the levels of these compounds within the brain, hence why they are sometimes called anti-histamine drugs.

For instance, if you are in a moving boat, airplane or car and stare at the floor or read a book, your balance system will still feel movement and send those signals to the brain. The eyes however see no movement and send a different signal to the brain.

Migraine sufferers are reported to be up to five times more susceptible to motion sickness. Interestingly, migraine medication (such as Verapamil) and some painkillers may actually help to reduce the susceptibility to motion sickness.

The neuron mismatch theory however has some problems, as it does not explain why certain motions do not cause symptoms while others do. However, tests on animals show a decrease in motion sickness sensitivity to some emetic drugs (lobeline and L-dopa), whereas vomiting following the injection of apomorphine was unchanged after bilateral labyrinthectomy (destruction of the vestibular systems, such as the cochlea). In addition, removing the vestibular projection areas of the cerebellum (nodulus and uvula) in tests has shown monkeys to be insusceptible to motion sickness. This would suggest that the inner ear is critical for the development of motion sickness.

-Two different types of Neural Mismatch
There are two main categories of neural mismatch identified that involves the sensory systems, being visual-vestibular and canal otolith conflict (vestibular- vestibular), each with two subdivisions. The first type of main category is when both sensory systems concurrently signal contradictory or conflicting information, and the second being when one system signals information while an absence of the expected signal from the other system occurs.

-Visual-vestibular conflict
--Type 1 subdivision
Visual-vestibular conflict occurs between motion cues provided by visual (eyes) and inertial receptors (vestibular apparatus). In the first type, the signals between the visual and vestibular systems disagree, such as being on a moving ship, car or airplane and you cannot see the surroundings to give you a visual reference that you are moving (or reading a map while moving), while your balance system informs you that you are in motion.

--Type 2 subdivision

The reverse can also happen, where the balance system informs the brain that the body is at rest, while the visual system informs the brain that the body is in motion, such as using binoculars or a telescope (normally with higher magnification). This is also called Visually Induced Motion Sickness (VIMS).

This type of sensory mismatch normally creates the worst symptoms and is difficult to prevent.

-Intra vestibular (Canal-otolith) conflict

Canal-otolith conflict is a mismatch of signals between information from the semicircular canals and receptors stimulated by linear accelerations. Visual stimuli are not needed for one to get motion sickness, as the blind can confirm. Further, at night or even with your eyes closed you can still get sick.

--Type 1 subdivision

In this situation, both the semicircular canal and the otolith organs receptors signal motion of the head. For instance, when you move your head as the vehicle is turning. Cross-coupled (Coriolis) stimulus results from the angular head movement while being exposed to sustained rotation about another axis. For example, if you were to sit in a rotating chair and nod your head.

The roll (semicircular) canals correctly sense the head movement as their sensitivity is almost not affected by environmental forces such as hypogravity (no gravity), orbital flight or hypergravity (enhanced G force such as tight turns in combat aircraft). The side-to-side sensors however sense incorrect head movement, resulting in neural mismatch, and the sensation can take up to 10 seconds to decay. In this time frame, while the canals generate incorrect sensations, the otoliths give correct information about head movement, creating a mismatch of signals that can be highly provocative.

The Coriolis effect can also happen when one is riding on a bad road or rough seas at a slow pace. Due to the poor road quality or rough sea, the vehicle will jerk and bounce and produce a sense of severe motion to the inner ear, yet due to the slow speed the eye does not sense the same proportional amount of motion.

People that are susceptible to motion sickness can experience symptoms (including vomiting) from only one head tilt through 90° in roll, while rotating in yaw at 30 rpm (normally on merry go rounds).

Repeated head movement even at slow turn speeds can induce motion sickness. This can be a problem on a scenic route with many long twists where one repeatedly moves the head to look at different objects of interest while the vehicle negotiates a long turn or series of turns. The same problem can be experienced when an airplane makes a long banking turn and one repeatedly moves the head to look at the scenery outside and then back inside. The faster the turn and or the faster the head movement, the easier one can get sick.

--Type 2 A subdivision

The second type neural mismatch for Canal–Otolith conflict is an absence of expected signals from the otoliths when the semicircular canals signal motion, normally space walk or reduced gravity (descending airplane or merry go-round).

This mismatch is due to the semicircular canals correctly sensing head movement in weightlessness, while the otoliths do not due to insufficient stimulation to sense linear acceleration. A change in ambient pressure (such as found in diving and airplane travel) can stimulate the semicircular canal receptors while the otolithic remains unassimilated, causing sudden vertigo (called pressure or alternobaric vertigo).

This mismatch is normally short-lived, unless one ear equalizes differently than the other, resulting in a feeling as if the world is suddenly turning. This can even happen on land where one suddenly experiences vertigo. A normal person equalizes their ears automatically about every 1 minute by swallowing. If the ears do not equalize in equilibrium, a mismatch occurs that can result in sudden vertigo.

---Positional alcohol vertigo (PAV)
This is another condition of type two mismatch of Canal-otolith mismatch.

Alcohol diffusion from the blood into the cupula renders it less dense than the endolymph, causing the semicircular canals to become sensitive to linear acceleration, and hence their orientation to gravity, that in turn can lead to the canals being selectively stimulated by movement, as the otolith is sensitive enough to pick up the same movement the semicircular canals normally pick up.

---Benign paroxysmal vertigo (BPV)
Debris that gets lodged on the cupula (cupulolithiasis) (called otoconial debris) can make it more dense than the endolymph, resulting in the same effects as PAV, heightened sensitivity of the semicircular canals to motion (normally motion involving moving the head to a right- or left-ear-down position).

--Type 2 B subdivision
In this instance, the semicircular canals do not signal any motion when expected to, while the otolithic and somatosensory Gravireceptors do, causing a canal-otolith mismatch in signals.

In this scenario a person is exposed to either rotation at a steady speed about a nonvertical axis, such as found in aerobatic maneuvers and fairground rides, or to repetitive translational (linear) acceleration such as a boat heaving, an airplane in heavy turbulence, or repeated braking and acceleration of a vehicle.

This kind of stimulation can be highly provocative and motion sickness symptoms can be experienced within minutes.

Poison response

The tests mentioned in neuron mismatch have led to a theory that motion sickness is a poison protection response. The mismatch of signals is seen by the brainstem (which detects neurophysiological dysfunction caused by neurotoxins) as neural dysfunction caused by poisoning. The body empties the gut to eliminate the poison from the system.

Even though the balance system plays a large part in motion sickness, one can still get sick due to other motion detection stimulation, such as pressure points on the feet and hands, mechanoreceptors in the skin, capsules of joints, muscles, and visual stimuli. Thus making head movements while the body is in motion (sometimes unavoidable such as in a small rocking boat or merry go round) normally will increase your susceptibility to motion sickness and make any symptoms you already have worse.

Simulator Sickness

Simulator sickness is thought to be due to the visual sensors picking up motion, while the other sensors do not provide the same expected signals such as gravity, pitch and roll.

The symptoms resemble that of motion sickness, namely nausea, vomiting, blurred vision, dizziness, vertigo, sweating, pallor and drowsiness, inability to concentrate, and can appear within 10 minutes of using the simulator. The first reported symptoms were from pilots using a helicopter simulator in 1957.

Some of the pilots reported sensory and motor disturbances that normally cleared within 12 hours, however some individuals experienced delayed effects lasting up to several weeks.

Individuals with no previous flight simulator experience had the highest susceptibility to symptoms, of which those that had higher actual flying experience were the most affected. This would support the theory that the body adapts to the neuron mismatch signals. Those with no flight simulator experience had no history of the neuron mismatch, and those who had actual flight experience would expect sensory input as maneuvers were done, such as gravity sensor input. The absence of these expected sensory inputs would create a greater neuron mismatch.

It should be noted that the quality of the display, the refresh rate of the screen, and whether the flight simulator had movement capability to simulate actual movement, greatly affect the susceptibility of individuals. The more the flight simulator resembles actual flight, the less susceptible individuals were to flight simulator sickness symptoms.

Virtual reality systems

Virtual reality systems are in a way very similar to flight simulators. They provide a visual input of movement. However, virtual systems rarely have any movement to them (unless it is large ones the participant can sit in). Many virtual systems are wrap-around glasses or helmets with displays inside to provide the user with a virtual world of movement. Here, the user normally has no frame of reference as provided by the aircraft cockpit in a flight simulator.

The quality of the visual display, its resolution, refresh rate and detail are normally far inferior to flight simulator displays and greatly affect susceptibility to symptoms.

In one study done with 150 subjects with 20 minutes of exposure in a virtual reality system, 61% reported symptoms of virtual reality sickness symptoms, which persisted even 10 minutes after exposure in some subjects. A big problem for virtual systems is the "lag" time of the system, or the time it takes the computer system to update and display changing visual images corresponding to the user's head movements. This "lag" time poses a challenge for the brain to handle and is linked to motion sickness.

Virtual reality sickness is basically the opposite of a person sitting in a moving boat and looking down. In the boat the body senses motion while the eyes sense no motion, and in the virtual reality system the eyes sense motion while the body does not, both are highly provocative to sickness.

It has been theorized that in virtual systems, the individual gets conflicting sensors as there are no cues for what is stationary and what is actually moving. Tests are currently being done to create virtual systems that have see-through displays. The user will be able to slightly see the background of the actual environment he/she is in while the screen output takes dominance. This visual cue will agree with the person's other sensors such as balance that the body is not in motion and may help relieve symptoms of motion sickness caused by virtual systems.

Space motion sickness

Cosmonaut G. S. Titov was the first to experience sustained weightlessness in orbital flight in 1961, and consequently the first to report space motion sickness symptoms.

It is reported that up to 70% of astronauts report symptoms in the first three hours of weightlessness when entering space. Some experience symptoms on return when gravity is experienced again.

Interestingly, the larger space vehicles where individuals could move about had a higher incidence of symptoms. This would agree with the neuron mismatch theory, where the visual sensors saw motion as the individual moved about, yet the gravity sensors sensed no motion as there is no gravity to affect them. It was also noted that individuals were less susceptible in subsequent missions, suggesting individuals adapted to the conditions.

Vomiting inside an enclosed helmet and pressure suit is potentially lethal, thus only individuals with no symptoms are allowed to do extravehicular activity (EVA).

A large concern is on return where disequilibrium can be experienced by some individuals when assuming an erect posture on leaving the spacecraft after landing as this can compromise emergency exit if needed.

Trains and motion sickness

Trains in most cases do not pose much of a problem to people when it comes to motion sickness due to most trains being very stable. Much research and design have been done to make trains give a smooth and silent ride. However, the quest for speed and getting passengers to their destination faster led to some unexpected problems.

Trains can only negotiate bends at a certain speed safely, however new designs made the suspension tilt the train cars by up to 8 degrees and resulted in around a 21% increase in speed. The result however was a marked increase in passenger discomfort and motion sickness. The tilting of the train caused passengers to experience motion that was picked up by the ears, but not by the eyes as the whole train tilted. The tilt angle was too small to be noticed from cues when looking outside the train; however the tilt was so fast as to cause the motion sensors to signal a massive movement.

Scientists at Mount Sinai School of Medicine led an international team of researchers (collaborating with scientists from Zurich University Hospital, Brooklyn College of CUNY, SBB, and Alston Schienenfahzeuge AG, a European transport company) in 2010 to investigate motion sickness on tilting trains that was requested by Schweizerische Bundeshanen a Switzerland train system. They found that adjusting the tilting of the train, motion sickness can essentially be eliminated. The timing of the tilting of the cars was adjusted when the cars enter and leave curves.

The first trains had a sensor in the locomotive in front that sensed the turn and sent a signal to the following cars to tilt. This caused a delay and resulted in the trains basically tilting in the turn. The resulted tilt in the turn is the same as driving around a bend and tilting your head and results in a neuron mismatch and possibly motion sickness as the gravity sensors are affected by the train turning.

The resolution came by tilting the cars just at the beginning of the curves by using a global positioning system (GPS) to sense the geographic position of the train on the tracks.

After publishing their findings online on July 25, 2011 in the Federation of American Societies for Experimental Biology (FASEB) Journal, SBB invested 3.2 billion Swiss francs for trains utilizing the results of the new technology.

Motion sickness vs sea sickness

Motion and sea sickness is basically the same, as both share the same symptoms and are thought to have the same causes (neuron mismatch). When people experience symptoms such as nausea and vomiting when on an airplane, in an automobile, or at an amusement park ride it is commonly called motion sickness, when the same symptoms are experienced on a boat or ship, it is called sea sickness; yet it is the same disorder.

Putting it all together

From the tests done on motion, it is shown that there is motion with six degrees of freedom on most ships, aircraft, and land vehicles. They are broken into two main divisions; angular and linear. In each division there are three subdivisions; pitch, roll and yaw for angular motion, and surge, heave, and sway for linear motion, with linear motion (heave) of the vessel creating the most sickness in the tests.

Thus, susceptibility is worse when a person sits or stands upright while the vehicle moves back and forth or accelerates and decelerates. This could be from looking forward while the vessel negotiates big waves and is slowed down as it climbs a wave, only to accelerate as it goes down the wave on the other side; or if one were to sit sideways on a boat that rocks side to side in waves. In this instance it would be best to lie down with the body facing the motion. From the figure below one can note the degree of susceptibility as motion changes in relation to body position.

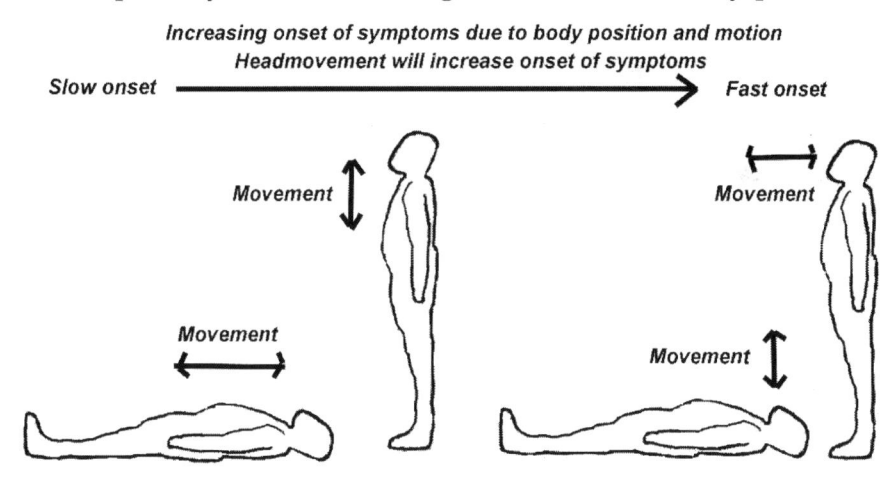

Increasing onset of symptoms due to body position and motion
Headmovement will increase onset of symptoms

Slow onset ⟶ Fast onset

Additional theories

Sensory and poison response are not the only theories for motion sickness, as other hypotheses for motion sickness are currently being investigated, such as the role of Coriolis forces (forces due to the earth's rotation) and other nonphysiological stimuli, including the role of the cerebrospinal fluid and the cerebellum. Motion sickness has even been associated with abnormal pacemaker activity in the gastric muscles called tachygastria.

Conclusion

It would seem then that there are a number of different possibilities and reasons a person can get motion sickness. This does not cure you of motion sickness, but may help explain why some remedies work for some people, and not for others. Thus, do not lose hope, keep trying until you find one or more remedies that enables you to travel without motion sickness symptoms.

Chapter 6

Preventing and treating motion sickness

As with everything in life, there is a scale. Most people fall in the middle when it comes to motion sickness susceptibility, with a few being highly susceptible to motion sickness and a few highly unsusceptible. The best way to prevent or stop motion sickness is to hug a tree, with the second best one to sleep under a tree. ☺

Note that it is better to prevent motion sickness than to try to cure it, because symptoms are hard to stop after they have started, however you can lessen the effect with medication and other techniques.

There are a number of advertised cures or remedies on the market claiming to reduce the susceptibility of motion sickness. Some have great results with scientific tests to back up their claims, while others are more based on a belief system. Due to the large degree of variance on what causes motion sickness symptoms in people, some remedies may work for one person and not another. Furthermore, a remedy may work in one situation, such as in a car or airplane, while failing to work on a diving vessel. This is due to additional parameters that may be present, such as diesel or gasoline fumes or exhaust smoke from the dive boat engine (two-stroke engine exhaust smoke is worst), the smell of fish or bait, and of other people getting sick.

In some situations, a combination of remedies may be needed to enable a person to function in the environment they wish to, without having symptoms of motion sickness, or reduce the symptoms to such a degree as to allow them to participate in the activity they wish to, such as scuba diving.

The only way to truly know if something will work for you, is to go and test it out for yourself.

Following is a number of remedies claiming to reduce the susceptibility to motion sickness.

Natural build up

The human body is a wonderful creation, able to adapt to a variety of situations. The body can adapt to motion and movement that will normally induce motion sickness, with symptoms frequently lessening or even ceasing after a few hours of exposure to motion. Natural build-up is preferred to drugs and other remedies as it is more permanent.

The body constantly evaluates sensory input to known experiences, when there is a mismatch the body tries to compensate. A short mismatch (such as tripping and losing one's balance) will cause an immediate response to allow one to regain one's balance. However, exposure to continued mismatch of sensory input requires remapping of known sensory experiences. Once the body has adjusted to the new condition, symptoms disappear. However, when conditions change again, such as returning to land, motion sickness symptoms can return for a short while as the body needs to readjust to the new conditions, called sickness of disembarking.

A future tolerance to motion sickness can be built up by exposing oneself to the conditions that would normally cause motion sickness to you (normally cross-coupled stimulation), only to such a degree before you get sick and then to change the conditions so as not to get sick. Over time the body will learn to adapt and each time a longer period may be tolerated until a degree of tolerance acceptable to the condition is reached. This can be done for instance by tolerating standing on a boat until slight symptoms are felt, then to lie down until symptoms improve.

One may also induce additional stimuli in conditions that would not normally induce symptoms, such as making head movements (side to side normally) while in an airplane while not in turbulence or being on a boat while the waters are calm. This will help build up a tolerance for worsening conditions of motion such as rougher waters.

There are exercises one can do at home, such as sitting on the edge of a bed (or standing upright on a solid floor) while rocking back and forth and making head movements until symptoms are felt.

Adaption and retention are very important for resistance to motion sickness. If the stimuli are small and the individual is capable of adapting very fast to the motions, then motion sickness is unlikely. If the individual's retention of the motion stimuli is good, then future exposure to motion would not cause undue problems. However, if the motion stimuli are more than the individual can adapt to, then motion sickness is likely, and even if the person adapts to the motions, if retention is poor then future motion stimuli would have the same effect as the first exposure. This explains to a large degree the differences in susceptibility to motion sickness in people.

Acupressure and acustimulation

It is believed that stimulation of the Pericardium 6 (Nei-Kuan) pressure point along the median nerve on the anterior aspect of the wrist can reduce susceptibility to motion sickness. See wrist band later in this book.

From studies done, wrist bands applying pressure on the Pericardium 6 point have failed to show any benefit for motion sickness, yet evidence from trials show a benefit to pregnant women against morning sickness and nausea and to people after surgery.

The failure to prevent motion sickness but help with surgery and pregnancy may be due to insufficient pressure from the band to compete with the neuron mismatch in motion exposure, as in trials done with cyclical manual pressure a reduced susceptibility was noted to motion sickness. Electronic wrist stimulation fared far better in tests, see Electronic wrist band later in this book.

Behavior modification techniques (biofeedback)

Although behavior modification has been tested and shown to have positive results in laboratories, the real-world results are not always the same. This is due to a variety of reasons, normally due to the instructor being absent and additional stimuli being present in the real world that are not normally present in tests, such as nausea inducing smells (engine exhaust smoke).

However, with training one can lessen the susceptibility to motion sickness and combining it with natural adaption is a good alternative to drugs, although it does take time and effort.

Behavior modification can be simple, where the person teaches themselves not to read a book or look down for long periods of time while in a moving vehicle or boat. Individuals can also teach themselves to be in the habit of looking at the horizon, staying in well ventilated areas, out of small spaces, and noting and avoiding foul smells.

Rehearsing the trip in your mind and mentally imagining yourself being happy and not sick before a trip can help. Try to anticipate the motion, if you know you are moving then your brain has one more signal agreeing with the sensors in your ears that you are in fact moving. If you think and believe you will be sick, you will be correct and become ill.

Exercises for motion sickness

As noted in the natural method, repeated exposure to motion may make one less susceptible to motion sickness.

Most military and air force training from different countries uses a habituation protocol to prevent motion sickness in their personnel when needed. The training involves a rotating chair that the participant is placed in and may be combined with visual stimuli to induce motion sickness and slowly build up a tolerance to it.

This training however is very expensive. A cheaper option that also uses a rotating chair and simultaneous optic illusion is becoming available, however with less motion stimuli than the military specs. Some habituation exercises can be done using only visual stimuli (visual-vestibular mismatches), called "times 2" and "times 0" viewing.

An additional exercise that can be practiced at home is available, called the "Puma method". The exercises were developed by Sam Puma (NASA flight surgeon) to assist pilots with motion sickness. This process can be very successful for the dedicated individual and is basically a habituation protocol where one repeatedly exposes oneself to motions that induce motion sickness. Almost like natural tolerance buildup, but with additional exercises.

For more information see **http://www.pumamethod.com**.

Ginger

Ginger (Zinginber officinale), a spice plant widely grown in the tropics such as Hawaii, the West Indies and Central America, has been used as an anti-emetic option as far back as 4000 years in Asia (Meyer, Schwartz, Crater, & Keyes, 1995), and a multitude of pills, herbs and drinks that contain ginger is sold under the premise of preventing motion sickness.

Many airlines, cruise liners and train chefs incorporate ginger into their foods for this reason. However, is this myth or fact?

Ginger in 250mg capsule form.

Trivia, the invention of the gingerbread man, a popular Christmas treat is credited to Queen Elizabeth I of England.

-Against Ginger

Amanda Elkins from Clemson University did a study where fifteen college students were given either ginger candies (980 mg of ginger), control candies (no ginger), or nothing as a control, and induced motion sickness using an optokinetic drum (a rotating drum covered with uniform black and white vertical stripes parallel to the axis of rotation that the subject sits in front of).

In her study, no significant differences of motion sickness symptoms were found, however other studies have found some symptom relief by using ginger.

In 1998, Gust performed a double-blind study on 44 students using 1 gram of ginger administered by liquid form (Sailor's Delight), like Amanda Elkins, he also induced motion sickness using an optokinetic drum. Gust also found no significant effect on the symptoms of motion sickness or tachygastria (rhythm in the stomach sometimes associated with motion sickness).

In 1991 Stewart, Wood, and Mims did a study by blindfolding participants and then placed them on a rotating chair. The participants also had to make timed head movements. An optokinetic drum was also tested. The study used 0.5 and 1 gram of ginger, and found ginger not to be superior to scopolamine (an anti-motion sickness drug) nor significantly different from the placebo group.

It should be noted that studies done where the subjects were in actual motion and not being tricked by visual imagery had better results as can be seen from the studies below.

Note, it is advised that ginger should not be taken two weeks before or after surgery if an individual is using blood-thinning medication such as warfarin (Coumadin).

It is believed that the ginger may interfere with blood clotting and could prolong bleeding time as ginger itself is a blood thinner. Ginger is also said to possibly inhibit an enzyme called thromboxane synthetase in pregnant women, this may influence sex steroid differentiation in the fetal brain. However, no study has currently confirmed any effects on the hormone by ginger. Lastly, ginger should not be taken with diabetes medications as it may decrease blood sugar levels.

-For Ginger

Mowrey and Clayson did a study in 1982 using 36 participants who were highly susceptible to motion sickness. Each was given 1 gram of powdered ginger root 25 minutes before being placed in a rotating chair. From the study, ginger was found to be superior to dimenhydrinate (Dramamine) without the side effects.

In 1989 Bone, Wilkinson, Young, McNeil and Charlton did a study on post-operative nausea due to anesthesia using 0.5 grams of ginger on 60 women who had major gynecological surgery. The study found significantly less nausea than those in the placebo group.

In 1993 Phillips, Ruggier, and Hutchinson did a study on the use of ginger for minor gynecological surgery on 120 women. The study found that ginger was effective in reducing nausea compared to the placebo.

In 1995 Meyer, Schwartz, Crater, and Keyes did a study to see the effects of ginger on nausea caused by chemotherapy using 1.5 grams of ginger in capsule form on 11 patients. The study found significantly less nausea when ginger was ingested before the therapy.

A study done on 644 cancer patients in 2009 found ginger supplements to decrease post-chemotherapy nausea by 40%.

A report from Obstetrics and Gynecology in 2005 on six clinical trials on 675 participants found ginger to be superior to a placebo and similar to vitamin B6 in relieving nausea and vomiting during pregnancy.

Various studies and experiments done on naval cadets found that ginger if taken in doses of 1 to 2mg before a trip did reduce symptoms of motion sickness.

Sea and Motion Sickness

-Why ginger is thought to work

It has been shown from many tests and experiments that irregular gastric contractions occur regularly if not always with motion sickness. During motion sickness, the CNS system (brain) releases a hormone called Vasopressin that causes your gastric system (stomach) to go into gastric dysrhythmias (irregular rhythm from the normal three cycle rhythm), making you ill. It has been noted that dysrhythmias starts about 1 to 2 minutes before you experience strong enough nausea to vomit and seems that this is the time the body said it's enough so let's vomit. The nausea strength has been directly linked to the strength of the gastric dysrhythmias.

Ginger is thought to interfere with Vasopressin release, limiting any gastric dysrhythmias that in turn may prevent nausea and vomiting. However, just as with motion sickness wrist bands, the effect they have can only override the body's signals so far, and eventually you may get sick with enough stimulation, especially if you are strongly susceptible to motion sickness.

-Conclusion on ginger

Thus, the debate of the effectiveness of ginger remains open, however in real-world experiences, especially dive boats, very favorable results have been shown by many people, including the author.

Note that people who dislike ginger may have the opposite reaction, and ginger may even enhance their motion sickness symptoms in this case, see Cephalic vagal reflex for more details.

It should however be noted that ginger does not totally make the user unsusceptible to motion sickness, it only lessens the susceptibility to it, and that ginger more affects the gastric motility rather than suppressing any neuron input.

Ginger should be seen as an addition to other methods such as natural adaption and peppermint oil; unless the person is already reasonably resistant to motion sickness or the condition only mild (such as calm waters or clear skies when flying).

Furthermore, note that ginger only seems to be effective if taken in doses of about 1 to 2mg and at least 25 minutes before being exposed to conditions that cause motion sickness, furthermore note that the effect of ginger only lasts for about four hours and more needs to be taken on long travels.

-Side effects of ginger
In most cases people normally have no side effects to taking ginger, those that do usually have mild side effects such as heartburn, diarrhea, and stomach discomfort.

Drugs

Note, if you choose to use medication for motion sickness, give it a trial day in advance to evaluate its effects on you. This is especially true if you will be operating any machinery or vehicles, scuba diving or sky diving.

Motion sickness drugs work by changing chemicals in your body (especially your brain) and normally blocking the effects of naturally occurring chemical histamine on your body (the reason it is also called antihistamine drugs).

Note that most drugs need to be taken half an hour to at least an hour before travel and in some cases it is recommended to start taking the medication the night before.

A variety of motion sickness drugs are currently on the market, with the most commonly used medications being antihistamines. Ones that are available without a prescription include dimenhydrinate (Dramamine®), meclizine (Bonine®), cyclizine (Marezine®), and sometimes the Transderm® patch.

Note, when you are self medicating with over the counter antihistamine medication, the normal accepted dosage is 25 to max 100 mg every 4-6 hours for adults with a maximum of 400 mg in 24 hours. Teens should be half this amount and children even less, for children under 12 years old one should not exceed 25 mg in four hours without a doctor's prescription.

-Promethazine (Phenergan®), (Pentazine)
Promethazine (Phenergan®) is a prescription drug that although it has antihistamine properties, it is chemically related to tranquilizers and as such is normally only prescribed when travel is needed and other methods fail. Promethazine can be intramuscular injected for severe motion sickness. However, note that as with most antihistamine drugs, drowsiness is a side effect that is worsened by the use of alcohol.

Even though Promethazine is a prescription drug, it is still one of the most effective anti-motion sickness drugs available and its effects can last up to eight hours.

Dosage is normally 25 mg for adults twice daily, however your doctor will specify the correct dosage for you. For children the dosage can be halved, yet note that this drug is contraindicated for children under two years old.

-Scopolamine-dextroamphetamine
Scopolamine-dextroamphetamine (combination of 0.4 and 5.0 milligrams respectively, taken orally) has been studied for use in space programs. Note that dextroamphetamine is a Schedule II controlled substance prescription drug and that the combination drug is not yet approved, thus any prescription obtained from a physician for this combination drug will be outside the FDA indications. Although the drug is very effective against motion sickness, the medication is still useful in situations for individuals performing complex tasks while being closely monitored.

-Scopolamine patch

Trans-Derm SCOP® (scopolamine patch) is an anticholinergic medication from the belladonna class and is widely used by scuba divers, fisherman and cruise ship passengers as it is found to be slightly more effective than Dramamine®.

The patch normally delivers 1.0 mg of scopolamine at a constant rate over three days. As such it is recommended for longer travels, normally over six hours such as cruise ships and long flights. In studies done by Dornhoffer in 2004, scopolamine was found to be the most effective prevention of motion sickness induced by cross-coriolis stimulation.

Note that the patch normally needs to be applied four hours before travel and that it is not well tolerated by children, nor should it be taken by the elderly (especially elderly with glaucoma or obstruction of the bladder neck).

Scopolamine (Scopace) or (scopolamine hydrobromide) is the pill form of scopolamine (duration normally six to eight hours). Since Scopace acts more rapidly than the patch form it is well suited for airline or automobile travel. Dosage normally ranges from 0.4 to 0.8 mg and should be taken on an empty stomach one hour before departure.

There are few problems reported with the use of the patch except for divers reporting 'dry mouth', possibly worsened by the dry air divers breathe when diving. Another side effect is visual disturbances.

Users may experience blurred vision after a day's use, worsening the longer the drug is used. The blurred vision can persist for some time even after removal of the patch.

Be careful not to touch the medication side of the patch, and wash your hands thoroughly after handling the patch. Touching the eyes (contact lenses) after handling the patch can severely irritate the eyes.

Additional side effects include hallucinations, confusion, agitation or disorientation, common in children and the elderly. Do not cut the patch to try and alter the dose as it disrupts the rate-limiting membrane delivering the medication. Individuals at risk for angle-closure glaucoma (caused by a sudden increase in pressure inside the eye, called intraocular pressure) should not take scopolamine.

Metoclopramide (Metozolv ODT, Reglan)
Metoclopramide is used to increase muscle contractions in the upper digestive tract to treat slow gastric emptying in people with diabetes (diabetic gastroparesis), which can cause nausea and vomiting. As the slow gastric phase can cause nausea, it may help with motion sickness.

-Ondansetron (Zofran)
Ondansetron belongs to the serotonin-family anti-nausea drugs and as such is a powerful anti-nausea medication, used to control nausea and vomiting after motion sickness has developed (normally by injection). Note that this medication does not prevent motion sickness or some of its related symptoms such as headaches and general unwell feeling. There are few reported side effects for this drug.

-Dilantin®
Phenytoin (Dilantin®) is an antiepileptic drug that has been shown to be effective against motion sickness, however it is not yet approved for the use of such. As all drugs, it is not free of side effects, yet it is a reasonably safe drug to use. Studies done on divers with dry chamber dives to 150 ft showed no change in susceptibility to nitrogen narcosis.

-Dimenhydrinate (Dramamine®), Driminate
Dimenhydrinate (Dramamine®) is used regularly to control motion sickness and nausea. The drug works like most other antihistamine drugs through the central nervous system to suppress symptoms.

Like most other motion sickness drugs it has potential side effects, normally drowsiness and impaired vision. Due to the drugs rapid onset of action, it can be used as a treatment of symptoms if no medication was taken beforehand. Good to carry a packet of them when you travel just in case you or a friend start to feel ill.

One to two tables for people 12 years and older every four to six hours if needed should do. For best prevention, take one hour before embarking. This drug can be found in a liquid form for children two years and up.

-Meclizine (Bonine®), (Antivert®), D-Vert, Dramamine II
Meclizine is similar to Dimenhydrinate. Dosage normally ranges from 25 to 50 mg for adults and should be taken one hour before departure. The drug normally lasts up to 12 hours, after which another dose can be taken if needed.

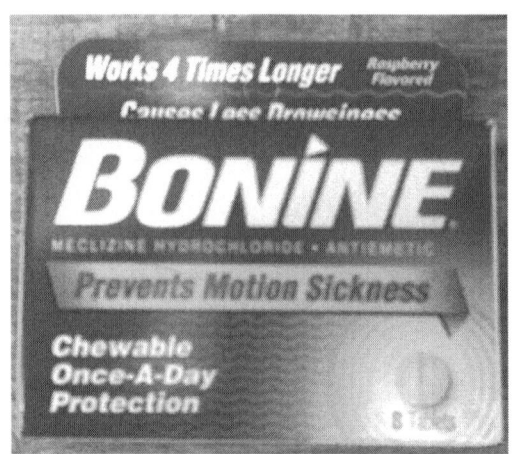

Bonine anti motion sickness medication, sold in many dive shops

Antivert is normally available by prescription only given 12.5 or 25 mg up to three times daily.

Bonine is normally available over the counter and many dive shops and food stores stock it, bonine is a lower-dose form of Antivert.

-Cyclizine (Marezine®)
Cyclizine is similar to Meclizine and Dimenhydrinate. Cyclizine is suitable for children six years and up and is mostly used for short trips and lesser motion stimulus such as automobiles.

-Diphenhydramine
Diphenhydramine is another antihistamine drug used to treat sneezing, runny nose, itching, watery eyes, hives, rashes, allergies, common cold, suppress coughs, motion sickness, to induce sleep, and to treat mild forms of Parkinson's disease.

-Haldol, Thorazine and Diazepam (valium)
These are anti-psychotic drugs that have dopamine blocking activity, making them useful for blocking nausea, in addition to stimulating the stomach in clearing food from the digestive tract (before you vomit it up ☺). These drugs work on the hypothalamus, pons and medulla oblongata to alleviate nausea.

-Diazepam (valium), Lorazepam and Klonazepam
These drugs are not normally used for motion sickness as they are sedating and addictive, however few people would have motion sickness problems when taking Klonazepam 30 minutes prior to the exposure. Diazepam is normally used to treat anxiety, seizures, alcohol withdrawal symptoms and muscle spasms.

-Alprazolam (Niravam, Xanax, Xanax XR)
Alprazolam is normally used to treat anxiety, panic, and depression. It may be helpful in treating motion sickness related to stress or fear of travel.

-Prochlorperazine (Compazine)
Prochlorperazine is an anti-psychotic medication and used to treat psychotic disorders such as schizophrenia, in addition to anxiety, and controlling severe nausea and vomiting.

Note on drugs for motion sickness
These drugs can have an effective reduction in motion sickness symptoms from a few hours to 24 hours or more, depending on the dosage taken. For many people, this may be the only way to enjoy travel without getting ill.

However, many of these drugs have adverse side effects, normally being: drowsiness, tiredness, dry mouth, inability to concentrate, irritability, scopolamine symptoms (confusion, agitation, rambling speech, hallucinations, paranoid behaviors, and delusions) (normally from wearing a patch), promethazine symptoms (twitching in muscles, breathing problems, impaired thinking and reactions and death (children younger than 2 years old)), restlessness, excitation, nervousness, insomnia, blurred vision; dry mouth, nose or throat; decreased appetite, nausea or vomiting, difficulty urinating, and irregular or fast heartbeat.

Allergic reaction to drugs can include difficulty breathing, closing of the throat, lips and tongue swelling, facial swelling and hives.

These drugs block a variety of signals and neurotransmitters creating the side effects, however as new discoveries are made in receptor subtypes, selective blocking of signals is possible, leading to fewer side effects for motion sickness drugs. Furthermore, note that only antihistamine medications that actually penetrates the blood-brain barrier are considered to be effective against motion sickness symptoms. Finally note that antihistamine drugs that are nonsedating have been shown to have no effect on motion sickness susceptibility.

Other medication

Even though antihistamine medication is normally the preferred treatment for motion sickness, there are other medications that may help to relieve some of the symptoms and can also prevent or lessen your susceptibility to motion sickness.

-Verapamil

Verapamil is a migraine medication and is sometimes prescribed for motion sickness, especially for migraine sufferers. People already taking the medication for migraines should consult a doctor before taking any other anti-motion sickness medication with this drug.

-Phenytoin and Carbamazepine

Phenytoin and Carbamazepine are seizure medications that may help in reducing the symptoms of motion sickness. As with Verapamil, consult a doctor before combining this medication with any other motion sickness medication.

-Buspirone (Buspar)

Buspirone (Buspar) and its alternative medication Beta-histine are anti-anxiety medications that may help with motion sickness, especially if the cause is stress related or fear of travel. See a doctor before combining these with other motion sickness medications.

Herbal treatments

There are a number of herbal treatments on the market, each claiming to prevent motion sickness without causing any of the side effects that normal antihistamine drugs cause. Most of these are a mixture of natural plant extract that are known to relieve nausea and headaches. Some of the most popular ones are:

-DizzyStop's®

DizzyStop's® has been invented by Otolaryngologist Stuart Barton M.D. The natural formula contains a combination of natural herbs designed to bring relief from motion sickness, nausea, dizziness and vertigo.

The manufacturers claim that the formula is superior or equal to prescription or over the counter medications and a safe, effective, non-drowsy, all natural and inexpensive alternative.
For more information see **http://www.dizzystop.com/**

-CanTravel™

CanTravel™ is a homeopathic remedy that relieves nausea, vomiting and queasiness caused by motion sickness, and is FDA registered, containing 100% natural homeopathic ingredients such as Pulsatilla, Ginger, Cocculus, Lactose, Peppermint and Kali phos. This product is in the form of pleasant tasting granules that are sprinkled on the tongue for rapid absorption.
For more information see
http://www.nativeremedies.com/products/cantravel-prevent-nausea-motion-sickness.html

-Trip ease

Trip ease is listed with the FDA for over the counter sale in the USA and comes in a 340 mg tablet form. Each tablet contains six homeopathic remedies effective in countering the effects of motion sickness.

The active ingredients in the formula are;
Borax, extracted from sodium borate and used to alleviate bad reactions to sudden movements such as turbulence while flying.
Cocculus Indicus, extracted from the cocculus berry and used to alleviate anxiety.
Gelsemium, extracted from the fresh root and used to alleviate dizziness, drowsiness and trembling.
Kreosotum, extracted from distillation of beachwood and used to alleviate nausea and vomiting.
Rhus Toxicodendron, extracted from fresh leaves and used to alleviate restlessness, nausea and vertigo.
Tabacum, extracted from leaves and used to treat sudden motion sickness, anxiety, chilliness and vertigo.

Additional ingredients are;
Sorbitol, a tabletting agent used in everyday items like biscuits and jams, especially diabetic jams. Tastes like sugar.
Magnesium stearate - E470b (vegetable sourced), a separating agent used frequently in tablets.
Sterilized talc - E553b, a lubricating agent used frequently in tablets.
For more information see **http://www.tripease.org**

-MotionEaze

MotionEaze is another natural herbal blend that contains ingredients to help control or prevent nausea and dizziness. The product is applied behind each ear on the soft area just behind each ear lobe where it is absorbed through the skin and thought to 'calm' the inner ear.

The product claims to work within five minutes and contains Lavender, Peppermint, Frankincense, Chamomile, Myrrh, Ylang-Ylang, and Birch.
For more information see **http://www.motioneaze.com**

-Hyland's Motion Sickness

Hyland's Motion Sickness is a traditional homeopathic formula to control nausea and dizziness, and stimulates the body's natural healing response to relieve symptoms.

The product contains:
Nux Vomica, helpful for sour stomach and nausea.
Tabacum, for "sick" headache with nausea and dizziness.
Petroleum, for nausea accompanied by a sensation of dizziness.
Cocculus Indicus, helpful for symptoms such as dizziness and nausea. The product uses a base of Lactose (milk sugar).
For more information see
http://www.hylands.com/products/motionsickness.php

-On The Move

On The Move is a blend of natural herbs to control nausea and other symptoms of motion sickness, including vertigo and dizziness.

The primary ingredient is Ginger Root, with additional ingredients being Licorice Root (for its gastrointestinal healing properties), Cayenne (for its pleasantly stimulating effect), peppermint, valerian root and catnip.

This combination of natural herbs can relieve the symptoms associated with motion sickness. For more information see
http://www.nomoremotionsickness.com/OnTheMove.html

Small snacks

Having a totally empty stomach can increase your susceptibility to motion sickness, and worsen any symptoms you already have, in addition to causing headaches. However, eating a large meal before a trip may not be a good idea if you suffer from motion sickness or if you are feeling ill. A better option would be to eat small snacks that are non-fatty or spicy over time.

Note that heightened motion sickness or susceptibility to it occurs about 90 minutes after consuming a large meal.

Cereal, oats bars, crackers, toast and ginger cookies that absorb excess saliva and settle the fluids in your stomach are good options. Green apples and bananas are good food to help with motion sickness if you cannot stomach dry snacks. However, do eat lightly before embarking on your trip, if you cannot eat anything, try sucking on a lemon or an olive.

Anything that will bind the fluids in the stomach to an extent to lessen the sloshing effect can help. The snacks will also help to keep your energy up while not being large so as to make you feel tired (medication and illness will probably already make you feel tired, you do not need additional help).

Fluids

For the most part, you want to avoid drinking strong coffee, alcohol, acid type drinks like orange juice and fizzy drinks if you are susceptible to motion sickness. Note that drinking lots of fluids at one time can cause a sloshing effect in your stomach that can worsen your symptoms. Drink small amounts of fluids (natural ginger beer or apple juice are good options) over time. You can also eat green apples to help settle your stomach while getting some fluid in.

Find a calm spot

Airplanes and ships can move in a combination of movements, however a study done from 1988 on vessel motion and sea sickness showed that vertical acceleration increased motion sickness symptoms more than roll and pitch acceleration.

Finding the part of the vessel where the least amount of vertical acceleration is, would greatly help, normally in the centre of the airplane (normally a wing seat) and the center of a boat, as the stern and bow are the points that will experience the most motion (bow is normally worse than the stern).

Think of a seesaw, the centre part moves very little while the people at the end of the seesaw bounce up and down. In addition to staying in the centre of the vessel, try to stay as low as possible while maintaining eye contact slightly above the horizon, or close your eyes.

Places you can try are: in a car use the front seat, on an airplane try the wing or more forward, and on boats try to place yourself in the middle of the boat (as low as possible while remaining well ventilated, on the top deck there is more air but also more motion), or at the stern if there is no exhaust fumes filling the area.

Get fresh air

Open some windows or try to stay in an area where there is a flow of fresh air. Fresh air will help avoid foul smells making you feel worse, in addition to helping lessen a claustrophobic feeling sometimes felt with motion sickness in an enclosed space. Try to deeply inhale and exhale through your nose to help lessen the nausea feeling. Note, face leeward (wind blowing away from you), so that when you vomit it gets blown away from you overboard and not onto you. If you are on an airplane, then increase the air blowing onto you and keep the vomit bag handy. In a car, try to sit by a window if possible.

Cephalic vagal reflex

Cephalic vagal reflex goes hand in hand with eating small snacks, especially non fatty natural fiber snacks. The body responds to the smell, sight or thought of food to ready itself for eating, or if it is foul smelling to stop you from eating it by making you sick and vomiting up any that you did eat.

The hypothalamus relays the sight, smell and thought signals to the medulla oblongata and then via the vagus nerve fibers to the stomach in order to stimulate the stomach into creating gastric secretion (digestive enzymes).

This process may inhibit motion sickness since it suppresses tachygastria, in addition to encouraging the stomach to remain in the normal three cycles per minute phase helping to lessen the effect of motion sickness and nausea. Note that food or smells that disgust you can have the opposite effect, making you sick. Tachygastria is a stomach phase with increased frequency of pacesetter potentials that disrupts gastric contractions and is associated with nausea and motion sickness.

In 1985 Stern, Koch, Leibowitz, Lindblad, Schupert, and Stewart did a study and found that tachygastria occurred in every participant who became sick when using illusory self-motion to induce motion sickness.

The conclusion is that anything (such as cephalic vagal reflex) that can lessen or prevent tachygastria and/or gastric disorder might also lessen motion sickness.

Electronic wrist band

Electronic wrist band

Electronic wrist bands are reasonably popular with travelers as they seem to work better than the pressure point wrist bands. The band works by sending a small electrical pulse through the Pericardium 6 (Nei-Kuan) pressure point along the median nerve on the pulse, the same point the pressure wrist bands use.

Most devices in this class have a strength setting to allow you to adjust the electrical signal strength to your needs.

The electric signals inform the brain to resume and maintain the stomach's normal movement and rhythm of three cycles per minute thus ignoring confusing signals from your normal senses. A small amount of gel is normally applied to the skin underneath the band to help with electric conductivity.

To keep the band in place, it needs to be reasonably tight, and by this action would assert pressure on the Pericardium 6 point in itself, the same as the pressure point wristband, with the added electric pulse making it more potent.

It should be noted that as with all other non drug-related remedies, the band does not make one immune to motion sickness, but rather more resistant to it, by either user belief and positive thought or actual physical workings.

Combining the device with other methods, such as ginger intake, smelling peppermint from time to time, and behavior modification such as looking at the horizon, one can greatly improve your resistance to motion sickness in a natural way.

Additional note, currently the devices are not waterproof and as such can be a problem for divers, especially if there is no time or dry space to store the unit when the diver needs to enter the water, nor will the device be of any help underwater.

Pressure point wristband (Seaband)

This is normally a wristband made from elastic or stretch material with one or two studs in the band. The idea is to apply pressure to the Pericardium 6 (Nei-Kuan) pressure point along the median nerve point, being about three fingers above the wrist joint. The theory is that this pressure point helps control nausea and vomiting by blocking nausea signals to the brain.

Unlike the Electronic version, this band does not replace the confusing signals from your other senses by its own signal, but rather just blocks the nausea signals out.

Even though these bands have been around for years, no actual scientific proof has been found, and in some tests applying acupuncture to this point contradicts the use of this point for nausea control by not being better than a placebo.

It should be noted that the placement of the band is very important as to the pressure it applies to the P6 point, in order to allow enough pressure to be applied to the correct point, and that the band is worn at least 10 minutes before embarking. A thought on the use of this band is that it is more a belief response from the user that helps with motion sickness control than the band itself. However, a study reported in the Journal of Midwifery and Women's Health notes that Seaband wristbands were found effective in relieving nausea in pregnant women.

Peppermint

Peppermint has some of the same calming effects as ginger on the stomach and the smell normally has a pleasant calming effect on the body. This may help to relieve symptoms of motion sickness and is a great addition to natural remedies such as ginger.

Obtain a small bottle of essential oil to carry with you. As soon as you embark, take a smell of the peppermint and again as soon as you start to feel a bit ill. You can also eat peppermint sweets to get both the smell and taste. You can also eat peppermint sweets to get both the smell and taste. Do make sure it is a quality brand that contains a decent amount of peppermint and is not just flavored. This is what I mainly used in my seven years as a dive instructor. I would suck on a peppermint sweet just before stepping on the boat, and would continue to do so during the trip. As soon as a guest started to feel ill, I had them sniff from an aroma therapy bottle that contained peppermint, and gave them a sweet to suck on. The effect is almost immediate, and helps a great deal. (Note if you are very ill, or very nervous, not much is going to help.)

Many captains like to use peppermint flavored gum to help with sea sickness, also keeps your breath fresh. ☺ Note lavender can be used if you do not like the smell of peppermint, although it is not as effective.

Ice water

Although this may not always be practical, unless your dive boat is in the Arctic or your plane crashed there (motion sickness is probably the least of your worries then), but it is reported that placing your feet in ice water may relieve some of the symptoms of motion sickness once you are already ill.

Coca-Cola and Pepsi

It is reported that these two beverages help control and reduce the susceptibility of nausea, this is apparently due to the caffeine and phosphoric acid in the drinks. Phosphoric acid is an ingredient in Emetrol, a drug to control vomiting.

Note however, the gas bubbles in the drink may cause burping that can cause you to vomit, it is advised to remove the gas (by adding a teaspoon of sugar to the drink) or by letting it stand for a while before drinking.

Hypnosis and self-hypnosis

In a study done with naval cadets and land based soldiers who needed to be transported, it was found that when they were told that it was expected they would get sick but that they would work through it and overcome motion sickness, they did. This theory is that mind matters and what you believe becomes true.

The option exists to have yourself hypnotized so that you believe you are immune to motion sickness. Your brain can be re-trained to stop travel sickness by teaching your brain to form a different set of expectations when you travel.

A less-expensive approach that you can do at home is to post notes and reminders all over for yourself (such as the bathroom mirror) that you do not get sick anymore. Alternatively, you can use a commercially available DVD or CD to listen to in order to re-train your brain. See **http://www.hypnosisdownloads.com/**

-Subliminal messages

Another approach if using a computer for daily work is to install a program that flashes subliminal messages on the screen. These messages are too fast to actually see, however your brain still picks them up. You can actually use this to make yourself believe anything you want. The theory is that if enough people tell you something about yourself, you will start to believe it and make it true yourself. So why listen to other people, tell yourself what you want to be yourself and make it true. This process is used extensively by the author. See
http://www.wordofmouthexperiment.com/dedpyhto/

Changing your handwriting

This may sound odd, but it works, and not just for motion sickness. The same theory here applies as in self-hypnosis, just more subtle. Our handwriting expresses who we are and our beliefs, that's why handwriting analysis can tell so much about you from just your signature. As you change as a person, so does your handwriting.

You can also reverse the process and deliberately change your handwriting to be the person you want to be. Each letter reflects an aspect of your life, and the combination, placement and size of letters and words affects your life.

By deliberately changing your writing style you can become more confident and change your life. This does take time to work, but it does work and is used by the author.

A good book is "Your Handwriting Can Change Your Life!" By Vimala Rodgers.

Chapter 7

Tips for preventing motion sickness

This section is to serve as a short and easy reference section to help prevent or lessen the symptoms of motion sickness. Some of the information is mentioned in more detail elsewhere in this book.

1: Find a well-ventilated area that has the least amount of motion, low and in the middle normally. On boats, find the mid of the boat, and on airplanes use the seats over the wings if possible. (Try to check in early on flights to select wing seats by a window to allow seeing out.) In a vehicle try to sit in the front of the vehicle, this allows you more room and a better view, including normally more fresh air.

2: Avoid reading while travelling if possible, or looking down at the floor, look at the horizon. This may be hard to get children to do, so play games like number plate guess or I spy.

3: Avoid foul smells or any smell that disgusts you, especially gasoline and diesel smell and engine exhaust fumes.

4: Avoid talking to or looking at people that are actively sick.

5: Think positive and try to calm yourself.

6: Avoid seats that are rear facing, and avoid looking back as the reverse movement from your perspective will make you more susceptible to motion sickness.

7: Avoid small spaces.

8: Eat bland food that is high in fiber, not fatty or spicy.

9: Try to lie down if possible.

10: Close your eyes, even for short periods of time to remove the visual stimuli input.

11: If you have to, vomit, rather than keep holding it in. Most people feel better after vomiting. This may involve asking the driver of a car to pull over, using the bathroom on an airplane or boat, or letting it go over the side of the boat.

12: Avoid alcohol and tobacco.

13: Although many people believe that drinking ginger drinks will help, avoid any drinks that contain gas (fizzy drinks). The gas in the drink can make you burp, not the kind of thing you want to do when you are trying to hold back from vomiting. Else remove the gas by placing a teaspoon of sugar in the drink or let it stand.

14: Try to avoid unnecessary head movement as this can make matters worse, especially no or low gravity situations such as in airplanes (turbulence, air pockets and fast maneuvers), spacecrafts and some amusement rides.

15: If you are the operator of the vehicle, try to make maneuvers such as cornering, braking and accelerating smoother and slower. Interestingly, the operator, skipper or pilot is normally the last one to get sick as he/she is so busy in steering that the thought of getting sick is not normally given much time. Try to steer yourself or keep busy with things to take your mind off getting sick. Listening to music will help as well.

16: Try to avoid rough conditions, if you are the skipper of the boat, steer to calmer waters if possible, and for cars stay on smoother roads where possible.

17: Do not focus on nearby objects, or on moving objects such as waves, other boats or vehicles, rather focus on distant objects such as the horizon or far ahead on the road.

18: Keep yourself busy, rather than thinking about how miserable you feel. Storytelling or even singing is better than sitting in self-pity. If you have an iPod or radio, listen to some music to help you take your mind off your ill feeling.

19: Eat small snacks low in fat and non-spicy, such as crackers, toast and ginger cookies. This works great for children who love to snack on travels. Crackers are far healthier than many chocolate bars anyway.

20: Try to avoid drinking too much fluid at one time as the sloshing effect in your stomach can make things worse.

21: Get a small bottle of peppermint flavor essential oil. Inhale some of the aroma from time to time to help settle your stomach.

22: Eat peppermint sweets to help settle your stomach, calm your nerves and give you a calming sensation, can also help mask foul odors that would make you sick otherwise.

23: Try some ginger before you embark and while on the trip. There are many forms available, however note that you normally need at least 1 to 2mg of ginger 30 minutes before you embark.

24: Try the electronic wrist band and see if it works for you, these have been reported in some cases to work better than the patch without the side effects.

25: Get rest; jet lag and tiredness may make you more susceptible to motion sickness, not to mention cranky.

26: If needs be, take medication to help you cope with motion sickness. There are a number of over the counter options to choose from.

27: Avoid standing if possible, standing makes you less secure and causes more body and head movement.

28: For toddlers, try to position the seat so they can see outside. This will normally mean a front seat or having the toddler seat positioned near a window in the back seat and not in the middle.

29: Fix your vehicle's suspension if it is not working properly, soft or incorrect suspension will make the vehicle sway more, creating more motion for the occupants.

30: Do not try to push through on trips, make frequent stops to give all a rest, and individuals prone to motion sickness time to recuperate.

31: Drinking caffeine, especially with anti-motion sickness medication, has been shown in some studies to help reduce the susceptibility to motion sickness.

32: For diving or fishing, prepare your gear before you climb aboard, if not possible then as soon as you are aboard, preferably while the boat is still moored up and more stable.

33: Avoid acid juices such as orange juice, rather stick to water, milk (note can make equalizing more difficult), apple juice or cranberry juice. Do drink fluid in moderation but do not let yourself dehydrate.

34: Drink some Coca-Cola or Pepsi, preferably with gas removed.

35: If your indigestion is really bad, take an antacid.

36: Sleep or lie on your back, it places less pressure on your stomach and supports the stomach better from bouncing around.

37: Have your ears cleaned before you travel. Blocked ears may cause one ear not to sense movement as easily as the other, causing an imbalance in sensory input. Cleaning your ears has been reported to reduce susceptibility to motion sickness as it allows the balance mechanism in the ears to work better.

38: Rest your head against the headrest if any to help keep it still.

39: Take slow deep breaths to help you relax. If you feel you are going to vomit, try taking a few deep fast breaths through your nose. This may stop or delay vomiting.

40: If using a train, try to take a seat near the front and next to a window, and do face forward.

41: For cruise ships, try to book a cabin near the middle of the vessel and near the waterline as this part is more stable. Try to in addition get a cabin with a window or balcony.

42: On a ship or boat, do not stare backwards, even if you look at the horizon, look forward as the reverse motion you sense when looking backwards can make you ill.

No matter how good the view to the back is, look forward

Chapter 8

Vomit in your regulator or not?

Many divers who get seasick and try to opt out of doing a dive are told that they will feel better once they are in the water. This can be true in some cases, however not always and may not be sound advice.

Once a person is sick, it takes time for the symptoms to clear. Even if the person feeling ill were to step immediately off the boat onto firm ground, the symptoms will still persist for some time depending on the severity of the symptoms. In addition, people get sick in the water the same as on the boat and can even get sicker underwater than on the surface, especially if they are already feeling ill.

Chances are that if the water is rough (rough is a loose statement and pertains to the individual feeling sick, definition of rough water), then the visibility may not be so good underwater. The combined effect of the movement of water, possible disorientation due to visibility, mask visual distortion, surge, neutral buoyancy (neutral buoyancy distorts gravity clues) and unequal ear equalization can make the person violently ill. This can be a real problem when you are underwater, how do you throw up underwater? In addition, anxiety can cause panic even in calm people and the possibility of drowning while throwing up underwater is a real concern.

If you have to

Vomiting underwater is actually an art, not one you would brag you are good at though. Regulators for the most part can deal with a great many things, including breakfast sometimes. My advice normally is to eat cereal or porridge as it vomits easier. ☺

-Taking the regulator out

If you take the regulator out of your mouth to vomit, you do not have the additional worry that the regulator may clog up, however you have a far greater worry, drowning. People have a tendency to vomit and expel almost all their air, then to take a sudden deep breath to make ready for the next cycle of vomit to come up. This can be totally involuntary and catch you off guard, causing you to swallow a lungful of water. If you are not panicking yet, you most probably will be now.

-Keep the regulator in

The second option would be to keep your regulator in and just vomit. As soon as you have vomited, just before taking a breath, press the purge button to clear the regulator. However, this does not always work as it does depend on what you ate and the regulator. Some regulators have mesh guards by the exhaust ports of the regulator to keep junk from entering the regulator, this can keep vomit from exiting the regulator. In addition, if your vomit is chunky and the regulator small, it may block the exhaust port.

An additional problem is that not all the vomit may be blown out, some may get stuck in the exhaust valve. This can cause the regulator to let water in when you are trying to breathe as the regulator exhaust valve is no longer sealing. In addition, you may breathe in any left-over vomit, making you even sicker if you do not choke on it.

-Swap regulators

This is normally the option I prefer to inform people to try, and use myself when I get sick. Here I normally swap to my secondary (alternate) regulator when I feel things are not going well, while holding my main regulator in my hand.

If I have to, then I vomit in the regulator and block the regulator opening with my tongue after every vomit so as not to take a breath from the regulator. I then quickly switch back to my main regulator to take a breath (remember to purge it clear of water before breathing). At the same time as I am taking a breath from my main regulator, I purge the secondary regulator clean. As the mouthpiece is now open to the water, the vomit can easily be blown out and does not need to go past the exhaust valve or exhaust port.

If I need to vomit again I switch back to my alternate that is now clean. This does take a bit more thought and coordination, but seems the best option for me.

Ultimately, you are the diver and will need to decide what you will do when you need to vomit underwater. The best would however be to make it to the surface and just let it all go, however that is not always possible, so now you have some options on how to vomit underwater. Wonder if anyone would be interested in an underwater vomit diver specialty? ☺

Regulator with exhaust valve cover may block vomit.

Chapter 9

Motion sickness and animals

Most people think that only humans have problems with motion sickness, yet almost all animals suffer from the same problem. Although Fido may not be going scuba diving soon, a ride to the local vet for a check-up may result in you cleaning the back seat of the car.

Pets show many of the same symptoms as humans to motion sickness including yawning, whining, signs of uneasiness or apprehension and diarrhea.

The following is some advice that may help you and your pet cruise around in style without needing to clean the car when you are done.

1: Do not feed your pet before going on a ride, not only can a full stomach make them vomit easier, they also have more to vomit and pooh. ☺

2: Animals, just as humans, can adjust to new motions, thus take your animal on short rides, gradually increase the distance of the ride.

3: Make sure your pet gets plenty of fresh air, possibly opening a window slightly so they can stick their nose or head out while you're driving. (Normally dogs, as cats seem not to be interested in this activity).

4: Make sure your pet can see outside, dogs love to watch the scenery pass by, cats however normally think they are the scenery and usually do not look outside. ☺

5: Place plenty of towels or old newspapers under your pets in case they vomit.

6: Try to calm your pet if they are anxious, normally if the only time they take a ride in a car is when they go to the vet, they will be afraid. They will associate the ride with a nasty experience. In this case take your pet for rides to a park now and again.

7: If your pet still has trouble, ask your vet to prescribe some anti-motion sickness medication for your pet. If you are really in a pinch, then you can use the normal over the counter antihistamine drugs such as Bonine, Meclizine or Antivert. The following is only a baseline, but for a puppy under ten pounds you can give 6.25 to 12.5 mg; ten to twenty pounds you can give 12 to 25 mg, and over twenty pounds a full tablet of 25mg, one hour before the ride.

Note however that cats have no histamine receptors in the chemoreceptor trigger zone (CRTZ) and therefore antihistamine medication is ineffective in treating motion sickness. Treatment for cats can be done with a α-adrenergic antagonist such as chlorpromazine. In addition, phenobarbital and diazepam can be used to produce a general sedative effect.

8: Anti-nausea medications that contain phenothiazine are most effective for dogs that develop motion sickness as a result of the physical motion, while providing sedation and inhibit drooling. Phenothiazine is a tranquilizer drug that antagonizes the CNS stimulatory effects of dopamine, thereby decreasing vomiting from many causes. However, note that they are stronger than anti-histamine medication and can produce side effects such as confusion and aggression.

9: Butorphanol is a very effective anti-vomiting drug for dogs receiving cisplatin chemotherapy.

Chapter 10

Tips for scuba divers

Although the tips section in chapter 7 covers some advice for scuba divers, there are additional tips that relate only to scuba divers.

The first thing to realize as a scuba diver is that sea sickness prevention starts when you plan your trip, not when you are on the boat. If you are prone to sea sickness, you may want to rather choose to do shore diving if possible. This will allow you to descend sooner and avoid unpleasant boat rides.

If you cannot or do not want to forgo boat diving, then try to book at times when the sea state is normally calmer. Weather conditions change during the year and sometimes the sea conditions are far rougher than other times. Ask the dive shop or boat operator the size of their boat and if they have different boats. Many operators who have multiple boats have boats of different sizes. Ask to be put on the largest boat they have and stress that you are prone to sea sickness.

Show up early at the boat so you can get the best seat. If you are taken to the boat by the dive shop, then try to get on the boat as soon as possible to get a seat with the least motion, normally in the middle of the boat. You may need to politely ask another passenger if they will swap positions with you, inform them that you are prone to sea sickness. If it is a multiday diving holiday and it is not a liveaboard, ask the captain or crew if they would reserve a seat for you for the full time you are there so that other divers do not take that position. (I find unwilling dive buddies are much more willing to move and give up their spot after you vomit on them. ☺)

Have your dive gear ready and in order before you get on the boat, as soon as you climb aboard start setting up your gear if possible. Do this if possible while the boat is still tied up on the dock, unless the boat gets launched from shore.

As soon as you kitted up your gear, find a calm spot and look at the horizon or lie down. If the boat is not casting off immediately, ask if you can wait on the dock until the captain is ready to depart. No need to unnecessarily sit bobbing on the boat. When the boat is in motion, try to stay clear of the exhaust fumes, other passengers smoking if allowed, and any other foul smells, this may include additional gas tanks, unwashed urinated wetsuits, dive gear smelling bad such as boots, other divers who believe they bathe every time they dive and do not need to wash up between dives, and other people getting sick.

Realize that the worst motion you can experience is when there is a forward and backward linear effect on your body while moving your head. This means that if the boat is moving over waves it will accelerate and decelerate as it negotiates the waves. This will push and pull your body forward and backwards and your head will also tilt up and down, looking around you will make matters worse. Thus when the boat is moving, sit down, face sideways while looking at the horizon, and do not look backwards as it will give you a confused sense of movement.

When the boat stops, waves will normally make the boat rock from side to side, now you want to face either backwards or forwards so that the motion hits you from the sides. This will help reduce head movement and conflicting signals. In bad weather however where the boat gets pulled on the anchor line, and the bow and stern up and down motion are bigger than the side to side rocking, choose the lesser one.

Sea and Motion Sickness

When you are ready to dive, get in your gear at the last moment if possible, yet try to be the first in the water. What you want to do is not sit around with heavy gear on, a weight belt and the sitting position press on your stomach. On that note, get a BCD with integrated weights as it will remove some pressure off your stomach. The motion you find in the water will normally be less than the rocking of the boat.

If you can, go down immediately, if you need to wait for other divers, ask if you can go down to around 10 or 15ft, 3 to 5m and wait there (if you are ok on gas consumption). If you cannot go down immediately, use your snorkel or, if you must, your regulator on the surface in choppy conditions so as to prevent you from swallowing water. Inflate your BCD so you can comfortably float and keep looking at the far horizon, do not look at other moving objects such as the dive boat, other divers or waves as this will give you a false sense of movement.

When descending, try to keep a visual reference, such as an anchor or descent line or sloping bottom. If not, look down at the bottom, if you can see it. While underwater, try to always keep a solid visual reference in view, such as the bottom, a wall or mooring line. This will help you fix up and down and help prevent vertigo and motion sickness.

People report that the tug of your weight belt will help for sensing up and down, true if you can concentrate on that and have one. Rather look at where your bubbles are going, or feel for them if it is low visibility or a night dive (should be able to sense bubbles hitting your hand even with gloves on). Putting water in your mask to see which way is up is a bad idea. Not only are you risking irritating your sinuses that will create more mucus to flush out the salt water and make equalization harder, you may also risk getting water down your nose and throat and can make you cough, vomit or panic.

After the dive, try to stay in the water rather than on the boat, this could be from letting other divers go up first or getting on the boat first yourself and taking your gear off to then jump back into the water in your wetsuit if possible. Just remember to remove your weight belt before you jump in if you are using one.

Back on the boat after the dive, change over to a new tank if it is a multi dive boat as soon as possible and then go find a calm spot, low down and not up the top deck. If possible lie down and close your eyes. In some cases a dive buddy or the dive operator crew or boat captain will be kind enough to change your tanks for you. Some dive operators do this as normal, some not. Check when you are booking if they do this and if you can request it as an option.

Use the tips section in chapter 7 in addition to these tips to help you get by. As soon as you get back on firm ground, go hug a tree ☺.

Thank you for taking the time to read Sea and Motion Sickness. If you enjoyed it, please consider telling your friends or posting a short review. Word of mouth is an author's best friend and much appreciated. Thank you.

End Note

Thank you for your purchase of this book. May it be a constant companion and an old friend on your journeys.

For comments please e-mail me at **antonswanepoel@yahoo.com** or **info@antonswanepoelbooks.com**

Anton Swanepoel

Resources

Web pages:
http://www.wisc-online.com
http://www.wiki.com
http://dictionary.reference.com
http://www.sciencedaily.com
http://www.ehow.com
http://www.dizziness-and-balance.com
http://www.medicinenet.com
http://summaries.cochrane.org
http://www.travelband.com
http://www.emedicinehealth.com
http://www.milfordanimalhospital.com
http://about.com
http://biobands.com
http://www.cdc.gov
http://www.hitl.washington.edu
http://www.essortment.com
http://www.nativeremedies.com
http://www.goddesscruise.com
http://www.charkbait.com
http://www.universalunity.net
http://www.umm.edu
http://www.tripease.org
http://www.mayoclinic.com
http://kidshealth.org
http://www.mdtravelhealth.com
http://www.webmd.com
http://www.motionsickness.net
http://www.scientificamerican.com
http://www.pppst.com
http://www.cruisesavvy.com
http://traveltips.usatoday.com
http://www.travelgearblog.com
http://www.motion-sickness.org
http://www.merckvetmanual.com

Spelling and grammar
Toni McNally
Ginger It! Software
WhiteSmoke Software

Other Books by this Author

All books are available for sale on Author's website; in Mobi, Epub, PDF, and Print form.

Sign up and receive news on new releases and book promotions.

www.antonswanepoelbooks.com

Laura and The Jaguar Prophecy (Book 1)
Laura and The God Code (Book 2)
Laura and the Spear of Destiny (Book 3)

Machu Picchu Doing It Yourself
The Art of Travel
Taking on The Road, Two Wheels at a Time
Angkor Wat & Cambodia
Vietnam Caves
Kampot, Kep and Sihanoukville
Motorbiking Cambodia & Vietnam

Dive Computers
Gas Blender Program
Deep and Safety Stops, and Gradient Factors
Diving Below 130 Feet
The Art of Gas Blending

Writing and Publishing Your Own Book

Ear Pain
Sea and Motion Sickness

Printed in Great Britain
by Amazon